ASHEVILLE-BUNCOMBE TECHNICAL INSTITUTE

NORTH CAROLINA
STATE BOARD OF EDUCATION

Y0-EAA-623

DISCARDED

AUG 4 2025

A Funny Thing Happened on the Way to the Crusade

A Funny Thing Happened on the Way to the Crusade

Lee Fisher

Creation House
Carol Stream, Illinois

© 1974 by Lee Fisher. All rights reserved.
Published by Creation House, 499 Gundersen Drive,
Carol Stream, Illinois 60187.
In Canada: Beacon Distributing Ltd.,
104 Consumers Drive, Whitby, Ontario L1N 5T3.

Biblical quotations are reprinted with permission
from the New American Standard Bible
© 1971 by the Lockman Foundation.

Printed in the United States of America.

International Standard Book Number 0-88419-043-9
Library of Congress Catalog Card Number 73-81981

Illustrations by Dwight Walles.

Foreword

Christians are human, and most of them possess a keen sense of humor. Contrary to the ideas of some, they are not prudes and prigs, but have a sensitive funny bone like anyone else.

I have asked Lee Fisher, my personal associate for over twenty years and a man who can see readily the funny side of any situation, to compile the humorous incidents which have occurred during our crusades through the years.

Lee authored one of the classic books of Christian humor, *Out of This World*, an account of the unique doings of his unusually dedicated father. Lee is just the man to do this book.

The incidents contained in *A Funny Thing Happened on the Way to the Crusade* will not only make you laugh; hopefully they will help you maintain a healthy sense of humor (one of life's most valuable assets) and see the bright, humorous side even to some of life's seemingly tragic situations.

May the Lord bless you real good!

BILLY GRAHAM

Preface

Humor is one of the delightful elixirs of life, and it is by no means the exclusive property of sinners. Saints have had their share of the spice of life. Consider Thomas More, who when mounting the gallows, said to the executioners, "Give me a hand on the way up. I won't need any assistance on the way down."

Carlyle once said: "True humor springs not more from the head than from the heart; it is not contempt, its essence is love; it issues not in laughter, but in still smiles, which lie far deeper. It is sort of an inverse sublimity as it were, into our affections what is below us, while sublimity draws down our affections what is above us."

True, the Bible says that "Every careless word that men shall speak, they shall render account for it" (Matthew 12: 36). But can words of humor be counted idle, when they cheer the human spirit and help us to see ourselves in our true light?

Jesus, the most exemplary man of all men, possessed a keen sense of humor. Why shouldn't He? He, who knew all men well, could see through their foibles, prejudices, and pretenses. He unveiled them so men could see how funny and ridiculous they were. One of his choice lines was "You blind guides, who strain out a gnat and swallow a camel" (Matthew 23:24).

Some people have the false impression that men of the cloth spend all their time saying prayers, reading the Bible, and telling people what not to do. I've mingled with show people and not a few comics, and I must say that the sharpest jokes, the funniest repartee, and the best storytelling I have ever heard came not from Shelley Berman, Buddy Hackett, or Jackie Gleason (who often use clergymen's warmed-over jokes) but from ministers of God. They have happily found what many nightclub entertainers have never discovered; a situation or a story need not be obscene or border on the double entendre to be humorous. Life itself is funny, and to see a tinge of the humorous even in the serious adds color and hue to existence on this pain-filled, sin-filled planet.

The best, most refreshing humor is not the contrived, well-rehearsed, ghost-written brand of the professional stand-up comics who often demand and get their $40,000 per week in Las Vegas and Reno. The best kind stems from normal situations which are ridiculously funny and hilariously amusing.

Billy Graham, with his zest for living and absorbing interest in the human scene, can be and is a serious, sincere man—when he is communicating the gospel. But those who know him personally will witness that the twinkle in his eye belies a love of repartee, a relish of good humor, and the fact that he is not above an occasional practical joke. His team meetings can swing from the ridiculous to the sublime, from the pious to the hilarious, in a matter of seconds.

A Funny Thing Happened on the Way to the Crusade lifts the curtain just enough to let you see the human side of the Billy Graham team.

Keep smiling. Remember, Solomon said, "A joyful heart is good medicine " (Proverbs 17:22).

Who's Who

Lane Adams is a former night club singer-turned-Presbyterian minister who was an associate evangelist from 1964 to 1973.

Don Bailey manages the team office in Atlanta.

Cliff Barrows, a Californian, has been Billy's musical director since he took time out from his honeymoon to lead crusade singing one night back in 1945.

Jerry Beaven was in crusade setup until the early sixties.

Ralph Bell is an associate evangelist.

Bill Brown coordinated the New York crusade and is now president of BGEA's film-making arm, World Wide Pictures.

Russ Busby is the team's official photographer.

John Cort is part of the crusade setup staff.

Lee Fisher is a long-time friend, researcher, traveling companion, and golfing partner of Billy's.

Leighton Ford, a Canadian, is an associate evangelist, a BGEA vice-president—and Billy's brother-in-law.

Billy Graham is the boss—a North Carolinian who began his ministry with Youth for Christ and was first noticed by the national media during the Los Angeles crusade of 1949.

Roy Gustafson, an associate evangelist, is the team's Mideast specialist, having led over forty tours to the holy lands.

Stuart Hamblen is the outspoken country/western singer who wrote "This Ole House" and "It Is No Secret What God Can Do."

Dr. Akbar Abdul-Haqq is a scholar from India whose work as an associate evangelist is largely on university campuses.

Willis Haymaker was the original crusade setup director; he set the pattern for advance preparation.

Howard Jones, another associate evangelist, concentrates his ministry to black audiences, both here and in Africa.

John Lenning is the man behind the production of each week's "Hour of Decision" radio broadcast.

Paul Mickelson was for many years crusade organist.

Carey Moore was an associate editor of *Decision* magazine.

Michael Ovikian is a U.S.-educated Israeli who speaks seven languages and is now the team's man in Latin America.

Dan Piatt specialized in the training of crusade counselors.

Charlie Riggs, from New York, joined the team in 1954 and became chief of counseling and follow-up three years later.

George Beverly Shea is a former insurance clerk whose baritone voice is a Graham trademark; he's recorded 39 RCA albums.

Tedd Smith, another Canadian, has been playing, arranging, and composing crusade music since 1950.

Walter Smyth is the vice-president for international ministries.

Don Tabb started out as a rodeo rider in his native Texas;

now he's a counseling and follow-up coordinator as well as pastor of the chapel at Louisiana State University.

Chuck Ward coordinates film and television outreach overseas.

Ethel Waters is the lovable blues-and-Broadway singer whose life was changed during the 1957 New York crusade. Since then she's been a guest soloist with the team.

Dr. John Wesley White is a Canadian-born, Oxford-educated associate evangelist and hockey fanatic.

George Wilson is the association's business and financial vice-president; he's no relation to Grady or T.W.

Grady Wilson is, in Richard Nixon's words, "a poor man's Billy Graham"; an associate evangelist and boyhood friend of Billy's.

T.W. Wilson, his brother, lives about a mile down the North Carolina mountain road from Billy and is his traveling partner.

Dr. Sherwood Wirt is a former newspaperman and World War II chaplain who has edited *Decision* since its beginning in 1959.

SHOW ME THE WAY
In the early days of Billy's evangelizing, he was holding a crusade in a rather small town. One morning he went looking for the post office. He met a boy about twelve years old and asked him the way.

Then, when he had gotten the directions, he continued, "Sonny, I'm Billy Graham, and I'm conducting a crusade in the football stadium. If you will come tonight, I'll tell you how to get to heaven."

"Oh, no," said the boy. "Any man who doesn't know the way to the post office wouldn't know the way to heaven. Thanks, anyway."

WAIT FOR THE BIG GUN
A Leighton Ford crusade in Halifax, Nova Scotia, was scheduled to wind up with Billy preaching the closing night. On the next to the last night, he wandered into the meeting (it was in an outdoor amphitheater) wearing sunglasses to keep from being recognized. When Leighton started to give the invitation to accept Christ, Billy approached a man standing at the back and offered to go forward with him.

The man glanced quickly at the blond-haired man with sunglasses and said, "No, I'm waiting for tomorrow night when the big gun is going to be here."

SAINT GRADY

During the Fort Worth, Texas, crusade in 1952, Grady Wilson acquired a ten-gallon cowboy hat of which he was very proud. Billy Graham, in a prankish mood, squirted a whole can of shaving cream into it and since the hat had white lining, the shaving cream was scarcely visible.

Soon Grady, late for a radio broadcast, rushed into his room, picked up his new hat, and plopped it on his head... and was on his way to the studio.

As he walked into the studio, Paul Mickelson was playing

"Sweet Hour of Prayer," the theme for the program. Grady hurried to the microphone and with a sweeping gesture lifted his ten-gallon hat from his head, saying, "Good afternoon, ladies and gentlemen. Welcome to the Billy Graham Prayertime Program." Resting atop his head was about four inches of shaving cream, shaped like a fallen halo.

Paul, still playing, gave Grady the cue that something was wrong with his head. Thinking his hair was uncombed, Grady reached up to straighten it. He immediately saw the station engineers bending over with laughter.

Grady quickly announced that Paul Mickelson was going to do some organ solos, and walked out. There was no devotional that day!

NO ROOM IN THE INN?

An inebriated man knocked on the door of one of the associates and asked, "Is this my room?"

The associate said, "No, sir, it's my room, not yours."

In a few minutes there was another knock at the door. The same man asked, "Could this be my room?"

"No," said the associate, "It's still my room."

The drunk then said, "Say, do you have every room in this hotel?"

LADIES' DAY

During the All-Scotland Crusade in 1955, Hugh Frazer, the department store tycoon of Glasgow, staged a gala luncheon for the team, his executives, and all the elite of the area. A team member sat as host at each table.

The room was overheated and the Scots, who are given to fainting in poorly ventilated rooms, were complaining.

Just as Billy arose to give his address, a corpulent lady slumped down in her chair at my table. A man jabbed me in the ribs and said, "Sir, you're in charge. The lady has fainted dead away, and you should get her out so she can get some air."

I arose with great trepidation, not wanting to distract Billy, who was having a hard enough time gaining the attention of his audience in the stuffy room. I put one hand under the lady's knees and the other around her neck. But she was heavy and limp, and as I tried to lift her, she began slipping out of my hands. In whispers I begged the man sitting next to help, but he was obviously hard of hearing and did not respond. Willis Haymaker, seeing my predicament, came from an adjoining table, and together we were able to get her up, over, and out.

Just as we were helping the lady to recover out in the

hall, the door swung open, and Grady Wilson came out with another fainting lady in his arms.

Later, back at the North British Hotel in Billy's room, he said to his team, "I want to thank you fellows for your help during that difficult luncheon. First I saw Lee going out with a woman in his arms. Then I saw Grady pick up another woman and carry her out.

"How was I supposed to deliver a serious address with you guys carrying on like that?"

A KICK IN TIME

President Lyndon Johnson, Mrs. Johnson, Ruth, and Billy were seated around a White House dinner table early in 1964. Out of the blue, the president asked, "Billy, whom do you think I should choose as a running mate?"

Before he could open his mouth, Billy got a kick in the shins from Ruth.

"Ruth," he said, rubbing his leg, "why'd you kick me?"

Ruth turned to Mr. Johnson with an embarrassed smile. "I'm sorry, Mr. President, but I believe Billy should limit his advice to moral and spiritual matters."

The president seemed to understand. But when the ladies left the dining room after the meal, he turned to Billy again and said, "Now, tell me what you really think."

THE ABANDONED PASSENGER

T. W. Wilson and Billy had arrived in Atlanta by plane in a terrible rainstorm. Their flight on to Asheville, North Carolina, was canceled. Having been gone from home several days, they didn't want to spend another night on the road, so they rented a car and started the 225-mile drive to Montreat. Billy was very tired and had just been released from the hospital in Honolulu, so he crawled into the back seat to sleep.

About fifty miles out of Atlanta, T.W. (we even shorten his name to "T" sometimes) pulled into a little truck stop to ask the quickest route to the Interstate. He quickly got out in the rain, got his information, and ran back to the car and took off ... not knowing Billy had gotten out to go to the rest room.

Billy came back, and suddenly realized he had been left. He went in the restaurant, thinking that T. W. would soon realize his mistake and return for him. But T. W. was innocently driving along, feeling content that Billy was able to relax so well in the back seat. Not until he got to Oteen, North Carolina, a town between Asheville and Black Mountain, did he try to waken his passenger. When he turned around and took a good look, his passenger had vanished! His first thought was, "Have I missed the Second Coming?"

Back at the truck stop, Billy was having problems of his own. Besides the rain, it was cold, and he had no hat or overcoat to offset the lingering fever. He ordered some soup to warm himself, then went to a pay phone to call his wife.

"This is a recording—the number you have reached is no longer in service."

He immediately dialed information and asked what was the matter with his phone number.

"I'm sorry," the operator replied, "but Mrs. Graham has had the number changed again."

"Well, I'm Billy Graham. May I have my new number, please?"

The operator had heard that line before. "Sure, you're Billy Graham! I'm sorry, it's an unlisted number." And no amount of evangelistic persuasion could coax it out of her.

Billy realized he was going to have to find his own ride. Finally he got a driver to consent to take him to Greenville for twenty dollars.

The two men crawled into the antique car, which looked like a trip to Greenville could possibly be its last, and took off, the rain pouring through the broken windshield. Trying to make congenial conversation, Billy introduced himself, saying, "My partner went off and left me. . .my name is Billy Graham."

The two incongruous statements so perplexed the driver that he continued on silently but kept a steady watch on Billy from the corner of his eye.

Thinking T. W. might have sent the state police after him, Billy kept peering at every passing car, thus further alarming his driver. When he tried to explain, the driver gave an unbelieving grunt, and Billy gave up.

Finally they arrived at the Greenville Holiday Inn. The manager-owner quickly recognized Billy. The driver watched unbelievingly as they greeted each other. When Billy paid the twenty dollars, the driver reluctantly conceded, "You know, I believe you really are Billy Graham."

In the meantime, T found it a little difficult explaining to Ruth Graham how he'd lost Billy, for Ruth thought this was surely his idea of a joke. It was no joke with T; he'd phoned the truck stop and learned Billy had left with some unknown driver.

Finally T went home, but arrived back at the Graham house considerably before Billy managed to find another way home from Greenville the next morning. By this time Ruth believed his story and thought the entire episode was hilariously funny. Billy eventually arrived to ask T the classic question, "What on earth happened to you?"

BONECRUSHER

Grady Wilson, nearly two hundred pounds, has often been accused of being Billy Graham's bodyguard. During the second London Crusade at Wembley in 1955, a man phoned and said he was coming to the Brown Hotel, where Billy was staying, and beat him up.

Forgetting the incident, Billy asked Grady to stand outside his door to keep out any disturbers during a press conference. Presently, a gruff, rough-looking man appeared.

"Who are you?" he asked Grady with a threatening voice.

Grady straightened his shoulders, stiffened, and replied, "I'm the man who cracks the skulls and breaks the bones of men who try to molest Billy Graham."

The man surveyed Grady's large frame once more, thought the situation over, and then said, "Good day," and left the hotel.

A FATAL MISTAKE

During the crusade in Memphis, Tennessee, the city's traffic safety department was launching a campaign for 100 days without a traffic fatality. The city officials asked for permission to put a neon sign on the crusade platform that simply said, "100 Days."

That night Billy thought the sign needed some explanation, so he said, "Of course we are delighted to cooperate with the traffic safety program in this city. You see this sign which says '100 Days'? It means the city is trying to have 100 days without a fertility."

HOW ABOUT SOME PRAYER?

During family devotions at the Graham household, Billy comments on the Scripture he's reading, and sometimes gets his finger jabbing the air as he does before the large audiences in his crusades.

One day little Ned became restless during a lengthy dissertation. Finally he raised his hand for permission to speak.

"Yes, Ned—what do you want?" asked Billy.

"Daddy," said Ned, "you said we were going to have family prayer. When are you going to stop talking and start praying?"

A TYPOGRAPHICAL ERROR

During city-wide crusades Billy usually prepares an advance summary of his sermon for the press. One night he was preaching on the immortality of the soul. A harried secretary omitted the *t*, so that the summary said, "What America needs is a new awareness of immorality."

One of us just happened to come into the office in the nick of time to save him the embarrassment of seeing headlines the next morning: "BILLY GRAHAM CALLS FOR MORE IMMORALITY."

OOPS! WRONG ROOM

When Walter Smyth, crusade director, assigned Don Tabb to escort Billy to the press room, Don thought he had said, "Take Billy to the rest room."

So Don took him down a long corridor, made two or three turns, and then led him through the rest room door. They stood there for an awkward moment; then Billy broke the silence.

"You don't mean to say that this is where we're going to meet those reporters!"

"Reporters!" Don said incredulously. "I thought Walter told me to take you to the rest room."

"No," Billy said, "I can usually find the rest room by myself."

SOLOMON'S GLORY

Quite a few years ago, Cliff and Billie Barrows decided to have a unique Christmas card. They made a picture of their four children (now there are five) clad in striped pajamas, singing and smiling as on Christmas morning. The card was sent to George Wilson with the request that he add an appropriate Scripture and have it printed.

As George looked at the picture, he had a diabolical thought. In the circle which Cliff had blocked out, he inserted this verse from the New Testament: "Solomon in all his glory was not arrayed like one of these." He had about six hand-printed and sent to the Barrows and a few of their close friends, letting them assume he had printed all of their Christmas cards this way.

As soon as Cliff and Billie received their card, they both got on the phone yelling, "Stop the presses!"

George calmly said, "But you said you would leave the verse up to me; I could find none more appropriate!"

CONVERTED DOGS

Belshazzar, the Great Pyranees dog who watched over the Grahams for nine years, was an impressive guardian full of surprises. His favorite pastime was to grab strangers by the arm, not harming them but nearly scaring them to death because he looked so formidable. One day, after he had seized an unwarned visitor, Ruth apologized, "I'm so sorry. It's too bad dogs can't be converted like people."

DON'T NAME IT

Bill Brown, former advance man and crusade director for the Graham association, took over as president of World Wide Pictures, the association's film company. While it is a very well equipped studio, it's not MGM or Warner Brothers.

One night Bill's older son asked, "Daddy, when boys ask what my father does, what should I tell them?"

"Just tell them your father is the president of a film company."

"Yeah," said the younger son, "but you don't need to tell them what film company it is."

BILLY MAY COME ON

Charles Allen, famous minister of the First Methodist Church of Houston, Texas, was given a new color television by his congregation. The first Sunday afternoon he eagerly turned it on to watch the Green Bay Packers play the Oakland Raiders.

Mrs. Allen saw him settling down in his easy chair and asked, "Dear, do you think we should watch football on Sunday?"

"No, indeed," said Dr. Allen. "But leave it on—Billy may come on any minute."

STICKY HONEY

When Mike Ovikian first came to the United States from Israel, he noticed how Americans like to use nicknames. He soon got used to being called "Mike" instead of "Michael."

Once when he was a guest at a couple's house, he was introduced to the housewife, whose name was Helen. However, during his stay he noticed that the husband always called his wife "Honey." Thinking that "Honey" stood for Helen, Mike began using the name as well . . . until Helen's husband made a few things clear.

BILLY GRAHAM PRESENTS

The television stations which carry Leighton Ford's one-minute devotional program introduce it as "Billy Graham Presents Leighton Ford with 'Insight.' " Jeanie Leighton was sitting in the studio lobby one day while Leighton was taping. Two high-school boys were there watching the monitor and trying to pick out the various TV personalities as they came through. They identified the newsman, the sports reporter, and the weatherman, calling out their names.

Then Leighton came walking through. Jeanie said, "Do you know that man?"

They looked Leighton up and down, and finally one of them said, "Oh, yeah, that's Billy Graham Presents."

THE INTERRUPTER

Billy speaks on Trans World Radio through his German interpreter, Peter Schneider. One day, a lady from Cologne wrote that she had heard Billy Graham preach and was impressed with his power and authority. "But there is only one thing wrong," she stated. "There's a man speaking English who keeps interrupting him."

THE HAPPY REVERENDS

Some team members were waiting in line at a cafeteria, laughing it up and having a good time as usual.

A lady watching them, who must have caught some conversation fragment about a crusade, said, "You men don't happen to be members of the Billy Graham team, do you?"

"Yes."

"Oh, no!" said the woman, "that's impossible! You're too happy to be preachers."

GRADY THE CANDIDATE

A political campaign was going on in the Lexington, Kentucky, area at the same time as Grady Wilson's crusade. One day, some pollsters for one of the parties were sent out to try to predict who was going to win the election. One of the men reported to his superiors, "We don't know who this Grady Wilson is, but by the number of bumper stickers we saw, he's running very strong."

IN THE POCKET

At Harringay Arena, where the first Billy Graham London crusade was held in 1954, a lady saw a man take a seat directly in front of her. In a few moments, another man, obviously a stranger to the first, sat down beside him. From their conversation, she found that they had several things in common: first, they did not like Americans; second, they did not care for services conducted by American evangelists. During the singing, however, they became quieter, and when Bev Shea sang and Mr. Graham got up to speak, they were almost reverent.

When the invitation was given it was clear that both were visibly moved. Suddenly, one turned to the other and said, "I don't know about you, but I'm going forward with the others."

The other looked at him unbelievingly.

Then the first said, "Before I go, I'd better get straight, so here's your wallet. I'm a pickpocket."

THE CATCHER IN THE AIRPORT
Billy and Ruth Graham had been in Florida for several weeks while Billy was recuperating from an operation. He was much improved and was preparing to fly north. He asked Ruth and me to take some of his luggage to the airport the night before so everything would be ready for the next day.

We loaded four bags into the trunk of the Graham car and headed for the airport. When we arrived, Ruth saw two strong-looking young men sitting on a luggage truck. Assuming they were skycaps, she said, "Fellows, could you give us a lift with this luggage?"

The men quickly rolled out the truck and loaded the bags. Ruth thanked them and handed them a dollar tip. But inside, she found the airline office closed for the night. The two men automatically gathered up the bags and returned them to the car, and Ruth opened her purse to give them another tip.

One of them blushed and said, "Please, lady, don't give me any more money. I'm embarrassed as it is. You see, I'm not a skycap. I'm a catcher for the Minnesota Twins. I just didn't want to refuse you when you asked me to help."

Ruth laughed and said, "Now, I'm the one embarrassed!"

Trying to save the situation, I asked, "Do you know whom you've just helped?" The catcher looked puzzled. I said, "Meet Mrs. Billy Graham."

"You've got to be kidding!" the ballplayer exclaimed. "Now, I really do want to give this dollar back!"

Ruth pushed the dollar away, saying, "Oh, no! I won't take it. That would ruin the story."

FIRST PRIZE

Years ago, Billy, T. W. Wilson, Grady Wilson, Merv Rosell, and Jimmy Johnson were holding a meeting in an old tabernacle in Raleigh, North Carolina. The weather turned cold and there was no heat in the building. Forrest Feazor, then pastor of the First Baptist Church, invited the young evangelists to move their service to his church.

"The young preachers were short on material," Feazor claims, "so each of them took about five minutes to exhort each evening. Then, when the services had concluded, my deacons decided to vote on which of the boys was the worst preacher. And, would you believe it...Billy won!"

THE LATE BILLY GRAHAM

At the European Conference on Evangelism in Amsterdam, a delegate handed Billy his Dutch Bible and requested his autograph. Billy flipped the front pages, looking for a blank space. The delegate now possesses a conversation piece, because Billy inadvertently signed on the page designated "Family Deaths."

SNAKES ALIVE!

David Stringfield, a friend of George Beverly Shea and vice-president of Baptist Hospital in Nashville, is known for his creative, imaginative pranks.

During the Atlanta crusade in '73, he walked into the crusade office and said to the secretary, "I'm Joe Hamilton, curator of the local zoo. Charlie Riggs made arrangements for me to supply the snakes for the crusade service tonight. And since we have this little cold snap, I decided I'd better bring them up here early. Is it all right if I unload them here in the office?"

Donna, a serious, sensitive girl, did not see the roguish twinkle in David's eye and said, "You better wait a minute until I check with Mr. Riggs!"

NO FORD IN HER FUTURE

During the Leighton Ford crusade in Melbourne, Florida, the publicity committee enlisted scores of people to distribute literature from door to door and give each person a personal invitation to the meetings. When the caller said, "We would like for you to attend the Leighton Ford crusade this next week," one elderly, partially deaf lady said, "Oh, honey, we've had a Ford for years and we like it fine."

"But I wasn't talking about a car—I wanted to invite you to come and hear *Leighton* Ford," said the visitor.

"Oh, you didn't get me, dear," the lady replied. "Ours *is* a late model. That's right, and we like it fine, thank you." With that, she closed the door.

BEV SHEA'S COMPETITION

The 1954 New Orleans crusade included a Prayertime broadcast each day. Bev Shea had gone to the beach at Gulfport one day to rest and stretch in the sun. Taking his radio with him, he was listening as Cliff came on the air.

Grady was prepared to bring the devotional thought, but during the program, he made motions to Cliff to announce that they would sing a duet. The only singing the two had ever done together was to harmonize a couple of times while en route to some crusade. Their one song was "Take Up Thy Cross and Follow Me." Cliff, busy with his announcements, nodded his approval.

It was a huge studio; Paul Mickelson was at the organ, Tedd Smith at the piano. During an organ interlude, Grady walked over to Paul and told him that he and Cliff would sing their song, "Take Up Thy Cross." Paul shook his head but, apparently unnerved at the thought of these two singing on the radio, pitched the introduction about three keys too high.

It was ridiculously out of their voice ranges. When they got to the chorus, Cliff put his hand over Grady's mouth, pushed him away from the mike and, in dulcet tones, *quoted* the words. When he finished, he explained to the listeners, "I'm not sure what key Mr. Mickelson had that song in, but it was too high for me."

Grady leaned over his shoulder and added, "Any key he puts it in will be better than that last one."

Then the two men started to laugh and could hardly finish the program. Back at their hotel, they found a waiting telegram from Bev Shea: "After hearing the rendition of 'Take Up Thy Cross,' I realize my job is in great jeopardy."

THE AMATEURS

Billy Graham and I were teeing off at Saint Albans Golf Club outside London one day. About twenty press photographers had gotten wind of the game and had arrived early to set up their cameras. Seeing them, Billy whispered, "Don't hit the ball too well—we don't want them to think we play golf all the time!"

LOST CONTACT

Cliff, Grady, and Tedd were conducting a prison service in a major city. After the sermon, Cliff announced the hymn of invitation. The piano was slow to start, and he noticed that Tedd was not up to his usual performance. Looking to see what was wrong, he saw Tedd in almost a kneeling position, playing the piano with one hand. For a moment he thought Tedd was unusually moved by the sermon; actually, he was bent over the piano keyboard trying to adjust his contact lens.

GOOD FOR ONE NIGHT

At Earls Court in 1966, a girl had been able to get a one-night-only ticket. She went forward that night and made a decision for Christ. The next day she went to the crusade office and said, "You gave me a ticket which reads, 'Good for one night only,' but I went forward last night and I'd like to be good from now on. Could I have one of those tickets which says, 'Good every night'?"

INAPPROPRIATE SELECTIONS

Cliff Barrows once chose "Heartaches—Take Them All to Jesus" to sing at a wedding. But Bev Shea easily topped that one when, in front of eighteen thousand people at Madison Square Garden, he sang, "I Come to the Garden Alone."

TAKEN BY SURPRISE

My father, Rev. Charles A. Fisher, was well-known by the team. He had a fatal bout with cancer which lasted about five years. Up to the last days of his life he conducted Bible classes for ministers, witnessed to the nurses and aides caring for him, and at eighty-two seemed determined to conquer the deadly disease.

One day, after the doctors had said he couldn't possibly live another day, Ruth Graham phoned me and asked, "How's your father?"

I reported that he had rallied again, to the astonishment of all.

Ruth exclaimed, "Isn't that amazing! When the Lord takes your father, He will have to take him by surprise."

ANYTHING TO PLEASE

A woman after a concert in Dallas came up to John Cort, an associate, and asked for an autograph. John was taken back, for few people had ever asked him for one. He felt sure the lady had made a mistake, so he asked, "Whose would you like? Billy Graham, Cliff Barrows, or Bev Shea?"

The lady smiled pleasantly and said, "Oh, I'd like Mr. Shea's, please."

So John signed: "Bev Shea."

NO DOGS, PLEASE!

Akbar Abdul-Haqq visited one of the team members in Montreat, North Carolina, when the cupboard was a little bare. Knowing that Indians are fond of hot food, his hosts served him a Mexican dinner, the hottest thing available. Akbar, always the gentleman, ate the food without comment.

That evening Akbar was among a few guests at the Grahams' for a picnic dinner. They served hot dogs with pickles, onions, and all the usual trimmings.

Staring at the wieners, Akbar asked one of the guests, "And what are these things?"

"Hot dogs," came the answer.

Akbar winced and said, "I ate Mexican food for lunch, but I guess I'll just have to pass on the hot dogs. Even the hungriest man in India wouldn't eat dog meat. I'm sorry, but suddenly I feel led to go on a fast."

QUICK-CHANGE ARTIST

In 1963, Billy Graham conducted three crusades in Germany: Essen, Hamburg, and Berlin. The team was small: Billy, Cliff, Carl Henry, John Bolten, and me. The night the meeting closed in Essen, Billy was very tired and wanted to get away as quickly as possible. His clothes were damp with perspiration as he finished preaching, but the five of us loaded into a car for the long trip to a hotel halfway to Hamburg.

"I've got to get out of these clothes or I'll be sick," Billy announced after we'd ridden a short distance.

Cliff brought the car to a skidding stop.

The busy autobahn was not the most ideal place to change one's clothes. But we made a circle around Billy as the cars whizzed by, and in minutes we were on our way to the hotel, a late dinner, and a good night's sleep. Not a single German, so far as anyone knows, was aware of the quick change.

SPREADING THE GOOD NEWS

At the Billy Graham Day in Charlotte, North Carolina, in 1968, Melvin Graham, Billy's younger brother, was given the privilege of saying a few words.

He opened with the story of the farmer who had seen the letters P and C in the sky; and being quite religious, he thought that surely meant, "Preach Christ." So he left his farm and started preaching. After a few fruitless months, he decided he had misinterpreted the letters; they must have meant, "Plow corn." So he went back to farming.

"I don't want to make that mistake here," Melvin told the large audience. "So Billy spreads the gospel, and I spread fertilizer."

CHANGING THE SUBJECT

Associate Evangelist Howard Jones was in Kewanee, Illinois, conducting a crusade. He was invited to participate on a radio talk show on the moral and spiritual conditions of the day. Howard observed that many young people were leading the way to a solution. As a case in point, he mentioned the Jesus People and the counterrevolution they were launching among the youth of America.

Then the interviewer said, "I think the discussion today has been very pertinent. Now we'd like to accept a few telephone calls from our listening audience and see what your thoughts are on the subject."

They waited for the phone to ring. Silence. Finally a woman came on the line. "I have a question to ask, although it's not related to the crusade or the moral revolutions in America."

"Fine, go right ahead," said the encouraging emcee.

"Well, I'm calling to ask if some of the ministers on your program could tell me where I could get eight pumpkins for our Halloween party next week."

PRETTY LOW DOWN
Many jobs in the Billy Graham Association are not as glamorous as people sometime imagine. John Lenning, an assistant to Cliff Barrows who helps make the tapes for "The Hour of Decision," said, "I'm so insignificant in the organization that it only costs a nickle to call me on a ten-cent pay phone."

WHAT'S THE NAME?
When the team was in Scotland in 1955, a young boy presented his Bible to Jerry Beaven, director of the All-Scotland Crusade, and said, "Could I have your autograph?"

Jerry wrote his name and handed the Bible back. The boy looked at the autograph in disbelief. His disappointment was quite apparent as he said, "You're not Bev Shea?"

"No, I'm Jerry Beaven."

The boy handed his Bible back. "Rub it out!" he demanded.

BUT IT FEELS SO GOOD
During the New York crusade, the team and friends gave Ethel Waters a special day at the Waldorf-Astoria Hotel. After listening to all the complimentary remarks, Ethel got up to speak. She said, "There ain't a person in the audience any more unworthy of this honor than I. But I'll tell you somethin', children, there also ain't no person here enjoying it more!"

APRIL FOOL

Judy Butler and Carol Roots served as secretaries to Bill Brown, director of the New York crusade, in 1969. Bill planned an April Fool's joke for Carol; he told Judy to hide in a closet by the Xerox machine and planned to tell Carol that Judy had her hand caught in the machine. However, he was delayed in carrying out the joke because an unexpected visitor arrived.

While waiting in the closet, Judy wondered if Bill might not be playing an April Fool's joke on her. But she stayed put. After several minutes, she heard Jack Cousins, an assistant to

Bill, as he brought a local minister into the room.

As Jack opened the door to the closet, he said to the minister, "Just put your coat in this closet while we talk." He started to hang up the minister's coat...and was startled and shocked to see Judy come squeezing out and leave without a word. She said later she knew her feeble explanation would sound worse than none at all, so she decided to let them find their own answers.

TO THE RESCUE

During the 1960 crusade in Sydney, Australia, a busload of people from the Outback were returning home and were at least fifty miles from any town when the motor began to miss. Finally, it broke down altogether.

Rain was pouring down. Finally, some cheerful person said, "There's no use sitting here doing nothing. Let's take our crusade songbooks and sing all the verses of every song until someone comes along to help us."

They were at page 49 when someone came with tools to help them. They were singing the last chorus of "Rescue the Perishing."

INFORMATION, PLEASE

T. W. Wilson went to his office one day and asked Elsie Brookshire, a secretary, "Where's the Encyclopaedia Britannica?"

"What's the rush?" Elsie questioned.

"Mr. Graham is speaking in New York on Ash Wednesday, and I want to be sure he knows the significance of that holy day," T answered. Painstakingly, he read the entry, then went to Billy's office and said, "Tell me about the meaning of Ash Wednesday."

Billy immediately responded, "Ash Wednesday usually comes about seven weeks before Easter, and it is when some Christians begin their Lenten observance. On that day, a Catholic Christian goes to church, kneels before the priest, and receives a smudge of ashes on his forehead in the form of a cross. As the priest does this, he says, 'Remember, man, that thou art dust, and unto dust thou shalt return.' The ashes are made by burning the palm leaves that were used on Palm Sunday the year before." With this recitation, Billy, who had just looked it up himself, paused and asked, "Is there anything else you would like to know?"

T turned and walked quietly out of the room.

MY BEST TO THE FOLK BACK HOME

Tedd Smith, pianist on the Graham team, is rather serious and dignified. One day, Jerry Beaven was seeing him off at the airport amid quite a large crowd of people. As Tedd turned to wave good-by from the steps of the plane, Jerry yelled, "I hope everything's okay back on the farm, Tedd! I hope the hens is layin' good and the cows is givin' lotsa milk!"

Tedd turned red with embarrassment. Jerry kept yelling, "And don't forget to mail that suit you're wearin' back to me! It's the best one I got, and I'll need it Sunday!"

STRAIGHTENING OUT UNCLE LEE

My wife Betty stayed with the Graham children when the rest of us went to Britain in 1954. I returned a few days early and joined the Graham household. The children were caught up with accusing each other many times a day: "You told a lie."

That evening at dinner, Betty tried to give a motherly lecture on the evil of false accusations. Everyone seemed very attentive and impressed.

Except two-year-old Franklin Graham, who was dawdling with his food. Just as Betty finished, I turned to him and said, "Franklin, you haven't eaten a bite of your dinner."

"Uncle Lee told a lie!" he announced with great glee.

The children roared with delight to see that Aunt Betty's lecture had been wasted on their little brother.

When all was quiet, I made a second attempt. "Well, Franklin, it's true. You haven't eaten a bite."

Franklin leveled his spoon at me and sounded forth again, smiling with triumph: "Oh, Uncle Lee tell a lie again!"

WHO? ME?

One evening during the same stay, Betty was tucking little Franklin into bed. He'd been particularly mischievous that day, and she asked, "Franklin, was anything special bothering you today? You and I don't usually have any trouble, but today you acted real naughty."

Franklin, at least fifteen years ahead of Flip Wilson, looked at her with the most innocent eyes and said, "Aunt Betty, I didn't do it!...The devil made me do it!"

WHAT ELSE!

Another night, Franklin had a bad nosebleed. Betty ran to his bedside and saw the blood spurting everywhere. Trying to fully wake up, she rubbed her forehead and said half outloud, "Let's see—what do I do for nosebleeds?"

Franklin was obviously disgusted that anyone her age would be so ignorant. "Aunt Betty, get a Band-Aid!" he ordered.

NEXT TIME

Mike Ovikian's driver's license expired while he was overseas. Back in Minneapolis, he went to take a new test on a snowy winter day when the roads were slippery.

From the moment the examiner and Mike met, they did not like one another. The officer looked as if he'd just had a fight with his wife. From the beginning, his stiff remarks shook Mike up.

At the end of the test the officer got out of the car and leaned forward in front of the hood. He asked Mike to put on the turn signals. Mike was so confused that instead of the blinkers he moved the gearshift. The car jerked and hit the officer's badge. Mike exclaimed, "Oh, no! Sir, I didn't mean to scratch your medal!"

"Scratching the badge is not as bad as running over my toes," retorted the officer. "For your next driver's test, I suggest you go to the other examining station in Excelsior; there the officers are better insured!"

THAT SONG WILL NEVER GO

During the Toronto crusade in 1955, Bev showed me a piece of music sent to him by Tim Spencer, a gospel singer and publisher. Bev liked the song. After sitting down at the piano and playing and singing it for me in the Coliseum one morning, he asked what I thought of it.

"It's okay, Bev, but I don't think it will ever go," I said. "In my judgment the words are rather prosaic and the music is somewhat of a steal from the old 'Aloha.' "

The song? "How Great Thou Art"!

Bev hasn't respected my musical judgment since.

THE GOLF FIASCO

Life magazine did an article on Billy when he conducted the North of England Crusade in Manchester. Among other scenes, they wanted some shots of Billy playing golf, and I was given the assignment to set it up.

There was a golf course a few miles out of Manchester where the team had been playing. So I didn't think I needed to make a special trip to make arrangements. I proudly and professionally organized the group, got them into cars, and started toward the course.

"I hope you have this all arranged," Billy said.

"Just leave it to me and don't worry," I assured him.

Chuckling, Billy answered, "Lee, that's just what I'm worried about. Things don't always come out right when you plan them."

This remark was prophetic. When we arrived at the course, it was swarming with golfers. They were having an interclub competition, and I was informed that under no circumstances could we go on the course.

"That's all right," I told Billy confidently. "There's another course just down the road. We'll go there."
About five miles further on, we came to the second golf course. Everything seemed fine but there was another hurdle to overcome. I had forgotten the golf clubs! I quickly assured the group that this was no problem; I'd go in and rent each one a set. But when I asked the pro for sixteen sets, he sadly told me that he had only *one* rental set! It was quite a day—four foursomes playing out of one bag, with *Life* photographers filming the whole ridiculous event.

WHAT'S UP, DOC?

Dr. John Williams, the minister of Saint Stephen's Baptist Church in Kansas City, Missouri, arrived at White Sulphur Springs, West Virginia, for the Billy Graham team meeting. When he got in the limousine to go to the Greenbriar Hotel, he asked the driver if he had seen Dr. Lane Adams, Dr. Howard Jones, or Dr. Grady Wilson.

The driver said he didn't know the men, and then asked, "Is this a medical convention here this week?"

Dr. Williams said, "No, I don't think so. There will be a lot of doctors at this convention, but they aren't doctors who can do you any good."

OUTSIZED MOSQUITO

Back in the "good old days" when T. W. Wilson, Grady, and Billy were selling brushes, they stayed in a cheap room in a little North Carolina town. T.W. and Billy had to share a bed. It was a hot summer night.

Suddenly mosquitoes swarmed the room, or so they thought. Billy said, "T, this place is terrible. I've never seen mosquitoes this bad." In desperation they pulled the sheet up over their heads to avoid the hungry insects. Billy kept slapping away, thinking that a few had stayed under the sheet.

Then he yelled, "Turn on the light. I've got the biggest mosquito that ever lived." T.W. turned on the light to see a giant bedbug. The mattress was swarming with bedbugs. They fled the hotel and found refuge in a vacant revival tent, where they slept on a soiled shirt spread over the sawdust.

BENEATH THE SURFACE

When team members conducted a crusade on the island of Barbados, a little girl was intrigued by the pale skin of the white team members.

"Why is their skin so much lighter than ours, daddy?" she asked. "They seem like such nice people. Why couldn't their skin be the same color as ours?"

The father said, "Honey, rest assured that although their skin is different, their hearts are just as black."

"GOD DON'T SPONSOR NO FLOPS"

When Ethel Waters was interviewed on a talk show in 1957, the emcee asked if she thought Billy Graham's New York crusade at Madison Square Garden would succeed. Ethel answered with her now famous quip, "Honey. . .God don't sponsor no flops."

THE "CHAUFFEUR"

When Billy and T. W. Wilson visited Princess Grace and Prince Rainier in Monaco, the princess had planned for the group to drive to Rome the next day to sightsee. Seeing a man with Billy, the princess asked, "Do you want to leave your driver here tomorrow, or do you want him to go along and drive your car?"

"Oh, he's not my chauffeur," Billy exclaimed. "That's T. W. Wilson, one of my associates."

THE LITTLE WHITE HOUSE

Ruth Graham and Ned were visiting us in Florida just before she joined Billy in Washington to be guests of the Nixons. We had a little guest house, which had been remodeled from a chicken house, where they stayed. Because it was painted all white with no trimming, we called it the "Little White House." It was comfortable, but the plumbing left a great deal to be desired.

On that particular visit, the bathtub drain refused to perform. Then, on the last night, Ned flushed the commode and it ran over, flooding the bathroom.

A few days after the trip to Washington, Ruth phoned my wife. She reported, "We had a lovely visit at the White House, and the plumbing was in perfect order." Then she graciously added, "But we enjoyed the Little White House almost as much as the big one."

THE BOA

During the New York crusade in 1969 at Shea Stadium, Billy assigned all his associates to parks and street corners for open-air services. Lane Adams was teamed with an Open Air Campaigner and sent to Washington Park. To get a crowd, the Campaigner used his artistic ability. Lane's job at that point was to hold the easel.

Unknown to the artist, a long-haired type with a band around his head stood behind him with an eight-foot boa constrictor draped around his neck.

Lane recalls, "I was grateful that the artist was going to speak first. When he turned from the easel to the audience, the snake was staring him right in the face. Without any hesitation he started to preach, his hands gesturing within inches of the reptile's mouth. After about five minutes of spirited speaking, hardly breaking the rhythm of his sermon, he looked at the hippie and calmly said, 'I see your snake, kid!' "

This so deflated the boy that he turned around, red-faced and embarrassed, walked away from the crowd, returned the snake to its owner . . . and came back to listen to the rest of the sermon.

RIGHT SERVICE, WRONG CHURCH

Howard Jones and his musicians went to a rest home for a service. They arrived at the scheduled time, but as they entered the lobby, Howard sensed that little preparation had been made for their coming.

When he found the lady in charge, he said, "Just call the group together and we'll begin the service." Although she looked a bit surprised, she gave the order over the intercom for everyone to assemble. As Howard was making his opening remarks a phone rang, and as usual the audience seemed more interested in the phone conversation than the speaker. So Howard stopped speaking until the conversation ended.

The lady in charge hung up the phone and said, "I'm afraid there has been some mistake. The woman who just phoned is from another rest home near here, and they have a crowd of people waiting for you and your team to conduct a service. I really didn't think you were scheduled to be here, but I didn't want to be uncooperative!"

OPEN MOUTH, CHANGE FEET

Leighton Ford has a sixty-second television program shown during the news on a number of stations.

In Charlotte, North Carolina, a woman recognized Leighton on the street and said, "Mr. Ford, you're so much better-looking on television than you are in person."

Leighton simply said, "Thank you."

Then suddenly a strange look came on her face as she realized how her remark had sounded.

"Oh," she said, "I didn't mean that! I mean just the opposite."

Leighton thought that didn't sound much more flattering, but again said, "Thank you."

"Anyway, I enjoy watching it," she went on. "Let's see. How long is it? It's five minutes, isn't it?"

"No, ma'am," Leighton said, "it's only one minute long."

"Oh, my," she answered. "It seems *much* longer."

Leighton decided it wasn't his day, tipped his hat, and said, "Good-by!"

GUESS WHO

During the Bluegrass Crusade in Lexington, Kentucky, Billy made the statement, "Some day Satan will become incarnate in a man. Just as Jesus was the expression of God, the Bible teaches that the Antichrist will be the expression of Satan. The Bible calls him, 'The man of sin,' and he will be filled with sin and evil."

A woman came up to him after the service and said, "I think my husband is the Antichrist."

"Why?" asked Billy.

"Because," she said, "if any man was ever full of the devil, he is."

CAT FOOD

T. W. Wilson and a quartet were traveling in France after the war as field representatives for Youth for Christ. They had all just graduated from college.

One night they were invited to a banquet to meet some important people in the area. They all looked forward to a tasty dinner, as meat was still very scarce. Everything went well until the main course was served, when T. W. noticed that the meat had a strange color and was especially tough.

After eating a bite or two, he turned to his translator and asked, "What kind of meat is this we're eating?"

Hunting for the right words, the translator answered, "I don't know how you say it. . .but it has four legs."

Alarmed, T. W. pursued, "But that describes many animals. Be more specific."

The translator suddenly smiled. "This ought to help. It goes *meow*!"

"*Meow!*" T. W. yelled. "You don't mean to tell me this is a cat!"

"That's it! Cat!" answered the interpreter triumphantly, proud that he'd found the right name in English. With that, he lifted the silver cover with a flourish. And there for T. W. to observe was the identifiable body of a cat!

PRAYER VIGIL

Chuck Ward was directing John White's crusade in Rapid City, South Dakota, and was urging the people to get involved in prayer. Emphasizing his point, he said, "It would be great if you would plan to pray around the *crock*."

In the outlying family areas, milk crocks were household items. An Irish-born minister spoke up, "Now, you're talking. This is the kind of prayer program my people would really back."

A BIG NOISE

A team member asked Canon Colin Kerr, "Just what is a canon in the Church of England?"

His reply: "Just as the name implies...a canon is a big shot in the church!"

FRIEND OR FOE?

When Billy and Cliff went to Germany for the Essen-Hamburg-Berlin crusades, Cliff didn't lead the music because the Germans insisted on using their own bands and choirs. Then, too, there was the language barrier. Cliff was content to operate the tape recorder, capturing the sermons for posterity. It seemed strange to the other team members to see Billy preaching in a crusade without Cliff's assistance in the music.

One night, Billy thought he should introduce Cliff. In his introduction, he told about Cliff being a pilot and how a commercial pilot had once allowed him to take over the controls for a brief time. Somehow the translation got mixed up and the audience got the impression that Cliff had been a bomber pilot in World War II. The German response was icy.

But the next night, Fuchida, the Japanese pilot who had led the attack on Pearl Harbor and who had since been converted, gave his Christian testimony. When Billy introduced Fuchida as the man who had led the air raid on Pearl Harbor, the German audience gave him a rousing, standing ovation! Lovable Cliff turned out to be a villain in Germany, while Fuchida emerged the hero.

BREAKING THE HABIT

On one occasion, Stuart Hamblen was to perform on the British Broadcasting Company's "Out of Town" show. One of the announcers asked before going on the air, "What are you going to sing, Mr. Hamblen?"

"I'm going to sing, 'It Is No Secret What God Can Do,' " Stuart answered.

The British announcer, with his waxed mustache and impeccable dress, replied, "Here in Britain, we don't make a habit of mentioning God in songs."

"Come on now, buddy," Hamblen reasoned, "don't tell me that when you sing 'God Save the Queen,' you hum the first word?"

That concluded the exchange.

TOASTING BEV SHEA

My wife and I had driven up from Florida for the wedding of Bunny Graham and Ted Dienert. We decided to stay in our Black Mountain cottage, although we had closed it up for the winter.

After the wedding and reception, Bev Shea said to me, "I'd like to go home with you and see your little house here."

I told him that we'd love to have him, so he followed us home. We visited for a time, then Betty suggested making some hot cocoa. Bev said, "That would be great. I just remembered that I missed dinner tonight."

Betty said, "Oh, Bev, this is terrible—we have hardly any food in the house. We've been eating out instead of buying very many groceries for such a short stay. Would toast help?"

Bev ate piece after piece of hot buttered toast and drank many cups of hot cocoa. I apologized again for our lack of food, but Bev just laughed and said, "That's all right, Lee. I've really enjoyed this. I like a good toast dinner now and then."

NO SHOES, NO MAGAZINE

Jean Wilson of the London office received word that a member of the World Wide Pictures crew was coming through. He had phoned her from Paris to say he would be arriving in London in about two hours and wanted her to have someone meet him.

"I'll meet you," Jean assured him. "But since we've never met, how will I recognize you?"

"That will be easy," he promised confidently. "Just look for a man wearing Indian shoes and carrying a *Decision* magazine." Jean rushed to Heathrow airport and took her place in the long line of people waiting outside customs hall. Her eyes quickly fluttered up and down as she checked the hands and feet of each emerging passenger. She saw a couple of people wearing what appeared to be Indian shoes, but neither carried the magazine.

She was so intent upon her assignment that she jumped when a strange man suddenly stopped in front of her and asked, "Are you Jean Wilson from the Billy Graham office?"

Looking quickly at the man's feet and hands, she answered, "Yes. But what happened to the Indian shoes and magazine?" Then as an afterthought she added, "And how did you recognize me?"

The man apologized, "I'm sorry—but I changed my shoes, and packed the *Decision* magazine in my suitcase. But it was easy to find you—I just kept looking for someone staring at feet instead of faces!"

A DEMON-MOTH

The night Billy preached on demons in Dallas, a man came to the first-aid room and said, "When Mr. Graham started to talk about demons, one flew on me." The doctor examined him; a moth had flown into his ear.

IT'S TRUE!

George Edstrom, now deceased, was for years George Wilson's assistant in the Minneapolis office. He was a rotund man of good humor and wit. One evening, he and Jerry Beaven were having dinner together. George had been seated in the restaurant, and before Jerry joined him, he drew the waitress aside and whispered, "See that big man in the booth over there? I'm taking him to the insane asylum."

As the waitress's eyes widened, Jerry hurried on, "Don't worry! He's harmless. But he does have suicidal tendencies, and I would appreciate it if you would take his silver away from him so he doesn't hurt himself."

Jerry then went to join George. Soon the waitress came, and while waiting for them to look over the menu, she reached down and picked up all of George's silver. He noticed, but thought she did it because it was dirty. But when she didn't bring him any more with his dinner, he became suspicious of Jerry. Not to be outdone, he proceeded to eat the entire meal with his fingers—confirming Jerry's story that he was demented.

WORKING FOR MAMMON
One day a friend asked Carey Moore's little six-year-old Jonathan what his father did. He rather proudly answered, "My father works for Billy Graham."

Immediately one of the other little boys piped up. "My daddy works for money!"

HE LOST HIS HEAD
A Billy Graham associate was preaching to a German audience through an interpreter. His subject was John the Baptist. When he told of John being beheaded because of Salome, the audience laughed uproariously. Bewildered, he asked the interpreter, "What's so funny about poor John being beheaded?"

The interpreter explained that he couldn't think of the German word for *beheaded*, so he'd told the audience that John's head had been amputated.

COVERING THE GLOBE

Mike Ovikian, elaborating on the distribution of *Decision* magazine in Latin America, said, "Our magazine goes to every country in South America—as far south as Tierra del Fuego, which is not too far from the South Pole. If we went any further south, we would need a Penguin Edition."

COMMUNICATIONS BREAKDOWN

During the 1967 London crusade, the eightieth birthday of A. Lindsay Glegg, a beloved English layman, came, and since he has been a great friend of the team for so many years, Billy thought it would be a good idea to have a supper at the hotel for him after the crusade service. He asked two team members to make the arrangements.

When they met with the hotel's assistant manager, they said they wanted a nice sit-down dinner with all the trimmings. One of the men suggested buffet-style serving to save time.

"All right, then," said the assistant manager, "a buffet dinner it is." The price seemed reasonable, so the three shook hands and the arrangements were completed.

But when the two came an hour early to check everything, there was a long table filled with every conceivable kind of alcohol—Scotch whiskey, gin, brandy, vodka, and just about every liquor the English could dream up. Waiters were busy readying ice, soda, and all the accoutrements for a drinking party.

"Look here!" said one of the Graham men, "this room is not where the Billy Graham team is having dinner, is it?"

"It certainly is, sir," came the polite, crisp, British answer. "And it looks like the Billy Graham team is going to have a ball."

The two rushed up to the manager's office. "What is all that liquor doing down in that dining room where the Graham team is meeting for dinner in a few minutes?!"

The manager said, "But you ordered a buffet dinner, didn't you, sir?"

"Yes, but we certainly didn't order any liquor! You should know that Billy's team doesn't carry on that way."

"I'm very sorry, sir, but there has been a misunderstanding. You see, in England, when you order a 'buffet dinner,' it means a deluxe cocktail party, and not a meal."

"Well," said the American, "in the United States a 'buffet dinner' means a meal, not a cocktail party. Please get that liquor out of our room and prepare some food for our people."

When the team came, all the liquor had been cleared away. The waiters brought in trays of hot canapes, and everyone thought that since such lavish appetizers were being served, a fantastic dinner was in store.

But to the disappointment and chagrin of the arrangers, nothing else was served. That was it!

When Lindsay Glegg, the guest of honor, arose to speak, he said, "My mother always told me not to overeat. On many occasions, I fear I have disobeyed her. But tonight I have followed her advice!"

INVESTIGATION COMMITTEE

When Billy was conducting a crusade in Oakland, the Christian students came up with a clever way of interesting the uninterested. They put a large sign on their bus: "Committee to Investigate Billy Graham." Under the large lettered words was: "Free transportation for anyone wanting to join this important investigation."

The buses were filled to overflowing every night.

SPIRIT AND FLESH

Mike Ovikian, director of Billy Graham's Buenos Aires office, is an accomplished linguist. He speaks seven languages, and he says that some Scriptures are not easily translated. "For instance, if you're not careful, the Scripture 'The Spirit is willing, but the flesh is weak,' can come out, 'The liquor is good, but the meat is bad.' "

REDUCED CREDIT

Billy was conducting a service a short time after he and Ruth had been married. When the usher came up on the platform and pushed the offering plate in front of him, he was surprised. With the congregation looking on, he reached for his wallet and pulled out what he thought to be a dollar bill.

As it dropped to the plate, he saw it was his one and only ten-dollar bill. His heart sank as he saw the bulk of his financial resources disappearing into the church coffers.

To further complicate matters, the church treasurer failed to give him an honorarium for his services that evening.

On the way home, he told Ruth what had happened. Instead of sympathizing, she said, "And just think—the Lord will give you credit only for the *one*. That's all you meant to give!"

A TOUGH REQUEST

Cliff Barrows had difficulty with the British idioms when he went to Harringay for the first British crusade. For one thing, he did not know that, to the English, *backside* meant "posterior." One night Cliff directed the audience to sing the song on the back page of their songbook. Very innocently he said, "Now, will you all please turn over to the backside."

A SONG IN THE NIGHT

At a counselor training session in Melbourne, Australia, a car in the parking lot hit a pole with a transformer on it, and the lights went out in the auditorium. A woman started screaming, and in the darkness a man called to Dan Piatt, "Sing some good old hymn."

Dan started to sing the only song that came to his mind: "Let the Lower Lights Be Burning." The audience laughed and happily picked up the refrain.

A VOLUNTEER

Most church folk in England are not accustomed to public invitations, in which the audience is asked to come forward and accept Christ. Grady Wilson was preaching in an Anglican church one Sunday and had the congregation sing a closing invitational hymn. Several verses had been sung with no one responding; finally, the vicar's wife stepped out.

Grady was elated. He shook her hand and asked about her need.

She answered sweetly, "There's no need! I just figured if someone didn't respond, this service would never end."

THAT WASN'T THE QUESTION
In Dallas during Explo '72 a Jesus person came up to one of the team members and asked, "Brother, are you saved?"

He answered, "Young man, I'll have you know I'm a member of the Billy Graham team."

The zealous teen-ager wasn't the least chagrined as he continued, "But I didn't ask you that!"

WANTED! PROFESSIONALISM
One night in the Dallas crusade, Ray Hildebrand, singer for the Fellowship of Christian Athletes, was featured. He told the audience, "As I stand before this great crowd of forty thousand people, I have never been more nervous in my life. This morning when I attended the Billy Graham team meeting, one of the members prayed, 'Lord, save us from professionalism.' When I heard that, I said, 'Lord, in my case—forget that! I need to be saved from amateurism.'"

IT TOOK AMERICA
One night at Earls Court in London, George Bev Shea sang "It Took A Miracle." A lady came up after the service and said, "You Americans are really something! We admit you are a great people; you beat us in a war and won your independence. But in my opinion that song you sang tonight is just going too far."

Bev, taken back, began to apologize. "I don't quite understand what you mean...."

The lady replied, "You sang, 'It took America to put the stars in place; it took America to hold the worlds in space.' Now, really, Mr. Shea, do you believe that?"

BILLY GRAHAM? NEVER HEARD OF HIM

It was a beautiful Florida moonlit night, the soft, humid air reminding Billy of the happy days he spent at Florida Bible Institute in his teens. After he and I had eaten dinner, he suggested we go for a drive before retiring.

I reminded him that I still had to type up the sermon he had dictated that day, as he had to tape it the next morning. Billy said, "Okay, you go ahead and type, and I'll go for a short drive."

About eleven o'clock, he still wasn't back. I finished my typing and went to bed. I had barely gotten to sleep when I was awakened by Billy's unusually noisy entrance. The strange look on his face alerted me, and I sat up in bed to ask, "Are you all right, man?"

With a look of chagrin, Billy answered, "Yes, I'm okay. I ran a red light! I was thinking about the perfect evening, and how well the car was running, and things like that when I heard this screaming siren. I looked in all directions, and in my rear-view mirror, I saw a police car with its lights flashing and signaling me to pull over. I couldn't imagine what the problem was."

I was wide awake by this time. "The patrolman sauntered up to my car," he continued, "and very matter-of-factly said, 'Let me see your driver's license.'

"I was still dumbfounded. I pulled out my billfold, found my license, and handed it to him without a word. He looked it over carefully, still with no comment or explanation. I was getting frightened. He stood there staring at the name William Franklin Graham, and I knew it meant nothing to him.

"In my mind's eye, I could already see tomorrow's headlines: 'EVANGELIST BILLY GRAHAM ARRESTED.' So I said to him, 'Did you ever hear of a preacher named Billy Graham?'

"I could see by the blank look on his face that he hadn't. He went on to say, 'No I don't believe I have; but I see by your license here that you're a reverend. Now, I'll tell you what I'm going to do, reverend. You see, you just ran that red light back there; but I'm just giving you a warning ticket and I want you to watch your step after this. I don't care who you are, you might get somebody killed running red lights like that.' "

WHO'S ON FIRST?

Dr. Harold Ockenga was introducing Leighton Ford to the Gordon Seminary students, and the slips he made were unbelievable.

(Leighton in reality is Billy's brother-in-law, having married his younger sister, Jeanne.)

"We are happy to have Leighton Ford as our speaker this morning. Perhaps some of you don't know that Leighton is married to Billy Graham's brother.

"Leighton is the man most likely to succeed Billy Graham as leader of the Billy Graham Association, and as many of you know, he is Billy Graham's son-in-law.

"So, now I present to you, Leighton Ford's brother-in-law, Billy Graham."

THE OTHER

During the preparation of the Dallas crusade, Charlie Riggs and his assistant, John Cort, arrived on the scene many weeks before the other team members, as usual. One Sunday, Charlie attended a church near his motel. The minister noticed him in the audience, but was having obvious difficulty remembering his name. Still, he was intent on recognizing him.

Finally he said, "Last November, two men from the Billy Graham team came to Dallas. One of them was John Cort, and the other is with us this morning."

MISTAKEN IDENTITY

People often confuse Billy with the evangelist of yesteryear, Billy Sunday. Once a man came up to Billy (who was then around forty) and said, "Billy, I'm certainly glad to meet you. I almost feel like I know you. I've heard my grandfather talk about you many times."

HAVE SOME POTATO CHIPS

In Lexington, Kentucky, during the Bluegrass Crusade, Billy, T. W. Wilson, and Grady Wilson were making a fast departure after the closing meeting. They sent Hank Beukema, then a member of Grady's team, for a sack of hamburgers and potato chips which they planned to eat on the way to the airport. In the rush of the final service, they'd not had time to eat lunch and were famished.

Hank got the potato chips, but in his hurry left the hamburgers on the counter. Imagine the men's surprise when they hungrily opened the sack of refreshments and found only an outlandish supply of potato chips.

THE FLYING SNAKE

Dan Piatt was training counselors for the Melbourne, Australia, crusade. One night, what seemed to be a black snake about eighteen inches long slithered through the air over the heads of the five hundred people. Women squirmed and some screamed; finally, the specter flew out of sight. Dan had just resumed his lecture when the strange creature launched another flight over the frightened audience. Finally he said, "We will take a recess, and I hope some of you men can capture that whatever-it-is so we can proceed."

A tall man stood on a chair when the strange creature once more glided across the room, twisting and turning like a reptile. He grabbed it and held it in the folds of a newspaper he had in his hand.

Dan finished his lecture and dismissed the audience. But the people crowded around him and said, "We're not leaving until we find out what sort of critter that was."

The man stepped up on the platform and unfolded his newspaper. Then he pulled out a giant moth which had gotten tangled in a long, black cobweb.

ORDERS ARE ORDERS

Both of the Wilson brothers are outdoor men. They love to fish, hunt, and tramp the woods. A few years ago, Grady happened to mention to George Wilson (no relation) that he wanted a fishing boat someday, but his wife, Wilma, didn't think they could afford it.

A few days later, George knew that Grady was in a crusade some distance from home, so he dictated a letter to Grady, trusting Wilma would open it . . . and she did.

I have checked with AlumaCraft boats, and they are sending the boat to Charlotte as per your instructions. They are granting you the 40% discount you agreed to. Please have $950.00 in hand, and $90.00 for the freight, because it is being sent C.O.D. This must be in cash, as they cannot accept a personal check due to the kind of interstate commerce regulation or something. Happy fishing to you!

Wilma called Grady in desperation. Tearfully she reminded him of all the things they needed around the house, their daughters' education, and how impossible it was for him to buy a silly boat at that time.

Grady had difficulty convincing her that it was all a practical joke of George's and that he had definitely *not* ordered a boat.

NOT A BAD IDEA

One evening at Chicago's McCormick Place in 1971, Billy mentioned a rumor that he wore three-hundred-dollar suits. After he said, "I never wore a three-hundred-dollar suit in my life," the crowd loudly applauded.

But Billy replied, "Don't applaud. I'd like to have one."

A GOOD START

When Martha Warkentin first came to Montreat to be Billy's regular secretary, she was as nervous as a lizard on a stove. After carefully sorting his mail one morning she started through the open door to his office, slipped on the threshold, and went sprawling to the floor, throwing all the mail into the room. Billy got up and helped her to her feet, saying, "When you deliver the mail, you don't fool around, do you?"

A few days later, she was determined to make amends. She entered Billy's office and said, "Would you like a cup of tea?" When she delivered it, Billy had a stack of letters spread out on his desk. Martha set down the cup, but her thumb caught in the handle, and the cup overturned and the tea cascaded over the mail on the desk.

"With a start like that," Martha told the other girls in the office, "things have to get better."

MY ACHING BACK!

During a Howard Jones crusade in Des Moines, Iowa, a group of ministers from the cooperating churches had been called together for a period of sharing and prayer. The minister in charge kept the participants on their knees for a lengthy time.

The next morning, a Lutheran minister said on his radio program, "I have a sore back this morning. The reason is: We had a prayer meeting yesterday, and we were on our knees for the better part of an hour. I guess I'll have to admit, I'm not physically prepared for such an unusual spiritual experience."

BE SURE YOUR FLATTERY WILL FIND YOU OUT

Once I was training counselors in the little Pike County town of Magnolia, Mississippi. My ego-pumping opener got me in trouble: "We're very thankful and proud of the contribution you people here have made to the upcoming crusade in Pike County. In fact, there's no place like Mongolia!"

STONED ANNOUNCER?

Don Bailey started in the Graham association as an announcer at Radio Station WFGW in Black Mountain, North Carolina. It's called the "Good News Station"; immediately after the news the announcers say, "And now for the good news—" and they quote a verse of Scripture.

It is reliably reported that one night Don's reading of the good news was "Let him that is stoned cast the first sin." Then he said, "Correction: Let him that is without stones cast the first sin." The third time he finally got the Scripture right: "He that is without sin among you, let him cast the first stone."

THE AMERICANS

When Woody Wirt, the editor of *Decision,* was in Paris, he went out with several of the team for a meal at a French restaurant. With much stammering and hesitation he laboriously gave the order for all the fellows in his elementary French.

When he had finally finished, the waiter replied in perfect English, "Will that be all, sir?"

LOVE THAT HORSEFLESH!

When Billy conducted a crusade in Lexington, Kentucky, he greeted the opening audience with these words: "I don't think there is any more beautiful section of the United States, unless it is western North Carolina where I live. When I drove through the beautiful bluegrass countryside today and saw the horses grazing in the green meadows, it made me hungry for steak."

THE GREAT IMPERSONATOR
In Dallas in September, 1971, Grady Wilson was assigned to a motel where Billy, T.W. Wilson, and I were staying. He arrived a day late, since he had to close a crusade of his own in a distant city.

Billy and T.W. were staying in a guest house at the Inn of the Six Flags, and Grady thought he would make a surprise entrance. He combed his hair down over his eyes and attached a false mustache to his upper lip. What he didn't know was that two suspicious men had been seen hanging around the cottage where Billy was staying, and security guards had been watching Billy's quarters since.

On my way to breakfast about seven o'clock, I saw this character with the hair over his eyes and the mustache loitering around Billy's door. I was getting ready to go phone security when I suddenly realized it was Grady!

"Man, what on earth are you doing in that disguise?" I asked incredulously. "There have been some suspicious characters around here, and you're fixing to get yourself shot."

Peeling off the mustache and straightening his disheveled hair, Grady said, "I was just going to surprise the boys."

A LITTLE RESPECT FOR THE ADMIRAL
Once when Tedd and Thelma Smith were attending a gala affair at one of Washington's leading hotels, Thelma approached a man in uniform, whom she took to be the doorman, and asked for directions to the ladies' room. He stiffened as if she had slapped him in the face.

"I'm sorry, madam," he said, turning away, "I don't work here—I'm an admiral in the United States Navy!"

THE ICE CREAM COMMERCIAL

Charlie Riggs was teaching a counseling class in Dallas. In making a point about being definite in dealing with inquirers, he said, "Now, if I just mentioned ice cream and said it was good, few people would rush out to buy it. But if I said, 'Tonight I bought some Baskin-Robbins Jamaica almond and praline ice cream, and it was the best ice cream I ever tasted,' someone might get excited enough about it to go out and buy some."

Afterward, a man made his way to Baskin-Robbins and ordered a large cone of Jamaica almond and praline. The manager, hearing his order, said, "I don't understand it. We've had the biggest run on those flavors tonight we've ever had. Someone must be giving us some free commercials."

A VERSE FOR BILLY

When Billy, with hair longer than usual, addressed the students at Southwestern Baptist Theological Seminary in September, 1971, he kidded Grady Wilson, who was on the platform with him, about being fat. Billy forgot to allow for the fact that Grady was to speak to the same student body the next day.

When Grady's turn came, he addressed the predominately short-haired assembly with, "A certain man I know, who spoke here yesterday (and I won't mention any names), cast aspersions on my obesity. If he were here, I'd quote the Scripture, 'If a man has long hair, it is a dishonor to him' (I Corinthians 11:14), and comment on it. But I'm a hunter, and I'll save my ammunition until the 'game' shows up."

NO WORRIES

Ethel Waters was in Los Angeles during earthquakes. After the quakes were over, Cliff phoned her.

"Well," Ethel said, "I was awed; but I wasn't scared none. I just said to the Lord, 'Jesus, You've got my address and I've got Yours; so there ain't nothing for either one of us to worry about.'"

THE CAR THIEF

In one crusade Russ Busby, the photographer, borrowed Walter Smyth's car to pick up some of the fellows from World Wide Pictures at the airport. Walter took the key off his ring and gave it to Russ.

When Russ got to the airport, he decided to check the trunk before picking up his passengers and all their luggage. He tried the key in the trunk; it didn't fit. He probed around in the glove compartment for a trunk key. What he didn't know was that a cop was watching his antics and becoming very suspicious. When Russ came around to the back of the car to try the ignition key again, the cop made his move.

"Is this your car, young man?"

"Why, no, it isn't."

"Well, I guess you'd better come with me."

"But, first let me explain," Russ pleaded.

He told him who he was and what had happened. The policeman seemed only partly satisfied and said, "I think we'd better go in and phone the owner of this car."

Walter was a bit disturbed because Russ had kept his car so long, and a need had arisen for it. When the policeman called him, he thought someone was pulling his leg, and when asked if he knew Russ Busby, Walter said, "Never heard of him in my life."

He then heard the cop talking to Busby and, realizing the seriousness of the situation, broke in. "Yes, I know him, and he's okay. Whatever he's done, short of murder, let him go."

IGNORANCE IS BLISS

Billy boarded a commercial aircraft and took a window seat. A man in a business suit took the seat beside him and when the plane took off and made the first turn, he nervously gripped the armrests, a look of fear upon his face.

Billy decided the man must never have flown before.

"Is this your first time on an aircraft?" he asked.

"No," the man answered, "I'm a commercial pilot. I work for this airline."

"Is that so?" Billy said, "Then why on earth are you so nervous?"

"This pilot nearly lost control on that first bank. Everyone else was calm because they didn't know what was going on."

HELLO?

A drunk phoned Walter Smyth. "What number is this?" Walter told him.

There was a brief silence as the drunk pondered the situation. Then he said:

"You've answered the wrong phone."

JUST HELPING THE CAUSE

When Grady Wilson greeted a group of old friends in the dining room of the Atlanta Internationale, he heard a familiar remark: "Grady, I believe you've gained a little weight since I last saw you."

Grady had a ready comeback: "Billy has a sermon on gluttony, and if he's going to use me as an illustration, I don't want to make him out a liar."

BOING!

Joe Emerson, a soloist, and I were on a plane between Barbados and Trinidad. He was studying Spanish, concentrating so hard that he didn't notice me switch seats with another passenger.

Suddenly Joe rapped the man in my seat on the head with a folded newspaper and yelled, "I've got it!"

"You've got what?!"

Joe looked up into the stranger's scowling face and said, "Uh, I've got real trouble—I thought you were someone else."

THE GREAT CROSS-CONTINENT RACE

In 1948, Cliff and Billy, following a crusade in Augusta, Georgia, decided to drive straight through to Modesto, California, Cliff's hometown and the site of their next crusade. They took Grady Wilson along, thinking that the three would take turns driving the two cars. Cliff's car had a disadvantage: he was pulling a trailer. So he started off first.

Billy and Grady passed Cliff about three hundred miles on his way, as he was having car trouble. The three talked the situation over and decided that since neither Billy nor Grady was a mechanic, the two would go on, and hopefully Cliff would get his car fixed quickly and meet them somewhere along the way.

In Albuquerque, New Mexico, Billy and Grady had car trouble, too; they told the General Motors garageman that their friend Cliff would probably be coming by soon with *his* car trouble. But since they had boasted that they would beat Cliff to Modesto, they didn't wait for his arrival. They drove night and day from Albuquerque and made the trip in what they called "incredible time." They were sure they were the winners by at least a full day.

Driving into Cliff's father's driveway, their sweet victory turned sour. Cliff's car, with the heavy trailer still attached, was in the drive. How they lost the race they still don't know.

CAN'T QUITE REACH

At the New York World's Fair in 1964 the Billy Graham pavilion was noted for its beautiful, huge water displays surrounding the building. One hot day an elderly lady asked Mike Ovikian if the pavilion had a drinking fountain. Mike teased her by saying, "Yes, ma'am, there's one on each side of the pavilion entrance."

A few minutes later the same lady returned. Huffing and puffing, she said, "Is there any way the fountains can be lowered so I can get a drink?"

SICKENING MUSIC

On the chartered plane to the World Congress on Evangelism in Berlin, I couldn't resist serenading the delegates with my Clavietta (an outsized harmonica). A clergyman was sitting next to me, and the air was getting a bit turbulent. While I played, he became airsick and vomited into one of the paper bags provided by the airline.

In Billy's welcome address to the congress, he said, "Many interesting things have happened enroute to Berlin. On one plane Lee Fisher decided to play a tune on his harmonica. But it didn't have the calming effect he had anticipated; in fact, a man sitting beside him became ill and vomited. I've always told Lee he's a better researcher than musician."

BATTLE OF THE BANDS

Another of my Clavietta concerts— this time on a chartered Korean bus from Pusan to Kwang-gu—prompted the driver to turn on his radio at full volume. I wasn't about to be drowned out; I finished my song, and the passengers applauded (whether for my stubbornness or because I'd finally stopped playing, I'm not sure!).

UPSTREAM

During the 1959 crusade in Australia, Grady Wilson was appointed to do the driving for Billy. Down under, they drive on the left side of the road as they do in England.

Grady had done an exceptional job switching to left-side driving. However, one day, he was engrossed in conversation and thoughtlessly pulled to the right in the face of a stream of traffic.

Billy threw the door open, jumped out and started running down the road. He couldn't be coaxed back in the car until we promised that Grady wouldn't drive anymore.

"It was just a lapse of memory," Grady pleaded.

"Yes, I know," Billy answered, "but many a lapse of memory has led to a lapse of living."

SUPPORT FORD

Several years ago Leighton Ford was conducting a crusade in Fredericton, New Brunswick. The Chevrolet dealer, a man with an evangelistic spirit, put a large sign on the front of his place of business. The huge letters said, "SUPPORT FORD." And underneath in small letters it said, "Support the Leighton Ford Crusade."

Addressing a civic club, Leighton quipped, "When Chevrolet supports Ford, that's real conversion."

NO SNOOZING

Howard Jones was preaching in a church in Liberia and became annoyed when a man kept walking up and down the aisles with a bamboo pole in his hand. At first he thought the man might be the "village idiot," but when he saw that he was accepted by the congregation, he tried to ignore the distraction.

After the service, he was told that it was the custom in that part of Africa to insure that no one dozed off to sleep during the service. The man with the pole had the authority to hit any sleeper on top of the head. Howard agreed it was a good idea, and wondered how he could introduce the practice in American churches.

DIDN'T EVEN TOUCH IT!

Mike Ovikian, like any newcomer, took awhile learning American slang. While visiting for a few days in a Minneapolis home, he teasingly told the housewife about some of the strange Middle East customs, which the lady could not believe. The next day the husband, tall and big, came to Mike and said, "Say, my wife tells me you were pulling her leg yesterday."

Mike, with a worried look, answered, "Oh, no, sir, I would never do such a thing to your wife."

ROUND TWO

One day Lane Adams had just completed a highly successful open-air service with an attentive crowd and a rewarding response when the man who accompanied him said, "See that big crowd on the steps of the old Treasury Building? Let's circle the block, and if we find a place to set up, we'll know it is the Lord's will to have a meeting there."

Lane, who doesn't consider himself quite the street meeting type, said that he never prayed so hard for a traffic jam in his life. But when they came around the block, lo and behold, there was a perfect place to set up for a street meeting.

Lane said, "As I began preaching, there was a burly, surly

fellow standing not more than six feet from me who kept making critical remarks, including some profanity and some unflattering comments about my ancestry. The more I spoke, the more personally he took the preaching and announced that he would personally take me apart right after the service. Under my breath I prayed, and much to my amazement began directing my comments right at this fellow.

"But it only increased his hostility, and he kept elaborating upon the bodily harm I would suffer as soon as I had finished. With that, I contemplated some sort of record-breaking filibuster, with the hope that the man might leave.

"About that time a black man asked me a question which indicated that he considered me a racist. To my surprise, the man who had threatened me throughout the service came to my defense. About that time, a third person began to take part in the fracas, and my somewhat vigorous effort to reconcile them availed nothing. The three-way argument became so heated that it was impossible to continue the service.

"By this time the attention of the crowd was drawn to the three men and not to me. It then dawned upon me that this whole development might be providential. So my colleague and I quietly folded up our gear, climbed into the van and drove merrily away, with the three fellows wildly waving their arms in the air and arguing at the tops of their voices."

A MATTER OF METERS

In Aarhus, Denmark, in 1955, Dan Piatt, advance man, went to the crusade arena to check on the platform one day. What he saw was unbelievable—a platform large enough for a skating rink, three times the dimensions he had given the carpenters. Eventually, he found that the Danes had taken the dimensions to be in meters, whereas he had intended feet. The Aarhus crusade broke at least one record: it had the biggest crusade platform in history.

BAAAH

One of Billy's researchers got him into trouble during the Seoul, Korea, crusade. Several people told him that Korea had no sheep (except on the southern islands), so he told Billy not to use any illustrations about sheep.

But one night Billy went ahead to preach on Luke 15—the parables of the lost sheep, the lost coin, and the lost son. He said, "Of course, you have no sheep in Korea. How many of you have ever seen a sheep?" To his astonishment, thousands of hands went up.

What neither Billy nor his researcher knew was that the Korean word *yang* can mean either *sheep* or *goats*. And there are plenty of goats in Korea!

TOO MANY SONGS

In the Miami crusade publicity an extra zero slipped in, so that I was credited with writing two thousand songs instead of two hundred. By the time we got to the next crusade in Los Angeles, *another* zero had been added.

Stuart Hamblen happened to be in the meeting one night and confronted me. "I don't believe you or anyone else ever wrote twenty thousand songs. Why, Charles Wesley only wrote six thousand."

"That was a typographical error," I explained.
"Well," snorted Hamblen, "I knew it was a big lie, whatever you call it."

TRY AGAIN

While preaching in the Portland, Oregon, crusade, Billy tried to say the phrase, "Hail-fellow well met." He was younger then and preached at lightening speed, and what came out was "a well-met hail-fellow." He realized that needed some correction, so he said, "A fell met male hellow." He went on from there to "I mean, a hell wet male fellow." By this time the audience was in an uproar, and he finished with "Aw, you know what I mean!"

THE POINT OF IT ALL

All the Graham family except Billy is Presbyterian. Although he is well-known as a Baptist, he attends Montreat's only church, which is Presbyterian, with his family.

One day Billy phoned one of his team members, "Come on up to our pool! I'm going to baptize four Presbyterians by immersion." After four Presbyterian young people had been baptized in an impressive ceremony and the benediction had been pronounced, someone said to Ruth Graham (who has always resisted immersion), "Ruth, I'd like to see you get immersed. Take me—I was baptized a Methodist by immersion."

Ruth answered, "Well, I was baptized a Christian, and that, I believe, is what it's all about!"

TWO MULLIGANS

T. W. Wilson was playing golf with Billy at the little golf course in Black Mountain. Billy's first ball went out of bounds. T. W., feeling pretty confident, said, "Hit a mulligan." Billy proceeded to hit the second ball out of bounds. T must have really been in a generous mood, for he said, "Aw, go on, hit another one, it's okay with me." Whereupon Billy hit his third shot within three feet of the pin. He made a two, and the generous T took a four.

Bragging, Billy said, "That was some deuce I had!"

Chafing a bit, T answered, "Yeah, but if I hadn't given you two mulligans, you would have had a fat seven!"

DULY SHOCKED

Once I spoke in a morning service in Manchester Cathedral in England. According to the rules of the Anglican church, I was not permitted to ascend the pulpit (not being an Anglican minister), but spoke from the steps back of the altar. I preached with typical American fervor.

I noticed an elderly lady tinkering with her hearing aid. After the service I made a point of shaking hands with her.

"Sir, I tell you, it was shocking," she replied. "So much so that I was forced to turn my hearing aid completely off. But I could hear you just the same."

HEART TROUBLE

In Sudan, near the east coast of Africa, Howard Jones conducted a service for a remote tribe in the desert country. Several hundred people gathered. He took his text from John 14:1, "Let not your heart be troubled." He noticed that the interpreter had a little difficulty with the text, but blamed it on the usual difficulties of translation.

After the service the translator said to Howard, "Did you notice me stumble over the first Scripture you used?"

"Well, yes."

Then his translator said, "You see, in the Sudanese language, the heart isn't the seat of emotions; the liver is. So when I translated your words, I had to go for this: 'Don't let your liver quiver!' "

A LITTLE DIVERSION

While Billy Graham was waiting to be introduced to the managers of the Holiday Inns of America in Memphis, George Bev Shea was getting ready to sing. On that occasion he used a small tape recorder for accompaniment. Billy watched Bev with interest as he turned the switches. Taking the machine for a radio, Billy leaned over and said, "I guess while I'm speaking, you'll be listening to the news."

HEY, BOY!

One summer in the fifties, Billy was speaking at Ocean Grove, New Jersey, at the Methodist annual meeting. Richard

Nixon, then vice-president, phoned one day and invited Billy and me to play golf with him and a friend.

I spent the rest of the afternoon practicing in anticipation. But when we arrived at the club the next morning, the vice-president said to Billy, "There's just one slight change: the owner of the club phoned and said he would like to play with us. So that poses a little problem, since you brought your friend."

Billy drew me aside and said, "I'm sorry about this, but you can walk around with us anyway. Why don't you carry my bag?"

We finished the first nine, and then Mr. Nixon said to me, "You come into the clubhouse and have a cold drink with us." As I started in with the foursome, the other caddies yelled, "Hey, boy! You can't go in the clubhouse. Caddies aren't allowed in there!"

SMUGGLING

Mike Ovikian, who's in charge of film distribution in Latin America, says that ridiculous custom regulations sometimes force him to smuggle films into certain countries. While traveling with him once, his pregnant wife, Marieluise, said, "I just hope the authorities don't take a look at me and accuse *me* of smuggling."

HE DIDN'T FIT THE IMAGE

When Howard Jones conducted a crusade in Liberia, he was invited to the office of one of the high government officials in Monrovia, the capital. When he introduced himself to the official, he was greeted with, "I can't believe you are Howard O. Jones, the radio preacher."

Howard insisted he was indeed the possessor of the voice that was heard all over Africa on ELWA. But still the man shook his head and said, "I just can't believe you are Howard O. Jones, the preacher."

Baffled, Howard asked, "Why do you doubt it?"

"Well, you see," said the man, "we believed that when Howard O. Jones arrived he would be an old man, a short man with a bald head and a big fat stomach."

Howard soon learned that Africans associated wisdom and experience with old age and its accompanying baldness and overweight.

A FLYING START

When Leighton Ford and Jeanne Graham (Billy's sister) were married, Billy was the natural choice to perform the ceremony in a large Presbyterian church in Charlotte, North Carolina. There were many dignitaries and civic leaders present for the formal afternoon affair.

Waiting for the wedding party to get organized, Billy and Grady Wilson were going over the service. The two old pros were obviously nervous. Billy put on the white gloves which came with his formal outfit. T. W. Wilson, who was also present to help Billy, said, "You aren't going to wear those in the service, are you? Why, you won't be able to turn the pages or handle the rings."

Billy obediently slipped them off.

About that time, Tedd Smith started to play for Bev Shea to sing his first number. Billy punched Grady and said, "Come on, that's us! Let's go out!" So before the wedding party had filed in, both Grady and Billy emerged in front of the pulpit during Bev's solemn solo, "I Love You Truly" . . . to the surprise of everyone.

Both men immediately realized their faux pas, so Billy, trying to appear nonchalant, smiled, nodded, and even waved to people in the audience. Grady stood stiffly biting his lip to restrain the laughter that welled up inside him.

After another solo, the wedding party finally marched in. Billy and Grady ceremoniously took their places back a few steps amid the palms and floral displays. Billy, appearing very formal now, articulated the vows for Leighton, telling him to please repeat, "With this wing, I thee wed."

Leighton was hard put to say the words, and an awkward pause followed.

Becoming aware of what he'd said, Billy corrected himself and Leighton quickly echoed the words before Billy could change them again. Laughter rippled through the audience.

As the service came to a close, Billy tried once again to redeem himself. With a confident, loud voice he said, "Inasmuch as Jeanne and Leighton have exchanged wings . . . ."

The audience really broke up this time.

Finally, the ordeal was over. Jeanne Ford was heard to say later, "The whole thing was such a comedy, I don't know whether we're legally married or not."

RABBITS AND BUREAUCRATS

Bishop A.W. Goodwin Hudson, on his way home to England, pulled our legs while speaking at a team meeting once. He said he wanted to share some of the problems and opportunities in the land of Australia, where he had just visited. One problem was the rabbit menace. He said Australia had a population of 14 million people, 140 million sheep, 750 million rabbits, and 750,000 public servants. The 140 million sheep, with the help of 100,000 people, produce wool worth 300 to 400 million pounds. The 750 million rabbits cost the country half as much as the wool clip. However, seven rabbits eat as much as one sheep. The 750,000 public servants cost the country nearly as much as the 750 million rabbits.

Mercifully, a powerful virus was discovered to keep the rabbits in check, and in addition sometimes a public servant eats a rabbit. Unfortunately, however, a rabbit never eats a public servant, and no way has yet been discovered to keep the public servants in check.

A WARM RECEPTION

In Maracaibo, Venezuela, Billy was invited to speak to the legislature. At the appointed hour, he, Grady Wilson, Cliff Barrows, and I arrived. While sipping coffee and talking to the president of the district, we heard gunshots.

The president jumped up, opened the door, and beckoned us to follow him. He seemed to realize immediately that the shots might be meant for him. As it turned out, a guerrilla gang had opened fire on the statehouse and were shooting the place up.

Somehow, we got separated. While running down one of the corridors, I bumped into Grady, who was looking for an exit. I had already found one, but had returned hoping to find the others. Grady said, "Well, man, let's not wait any longer. We've got to get out of here!"

The door opened on a street, and as we peeked out, a taxi approached. I gave the shrillest cab whistle I could muster, and he came to a grinding halt in front of us.

Once inside the cab, we were both thanking the Lord for our safe escape but lamenting that we had had to leave Billy and Cliff. But our concern was quickly erased when we arrived at the hotel. They had beaten us back and both were unharmed. The president had been provided an escape car and the three of them had sped away to safety.

That was one speech Billy never got to deliver. The revolution had preempted his talk.

WHAT HAPPENED, BOSS?

George Wilson was showing some board members through the spacious Minneapolis office. George takes great pride in the fact that he knows how to operate every machine in the building. While demonstrating the tying machine, he leaned over a bit too far, and his necktie got caught. He was unable to extricate it, and an employee finally had to cut it off just below the knot. In typical George Wilson fashion, he proceeded nonchalantly on his tour of the office, looking like a mini-version of Colonel Sanders.

I HAVE BEEN TO THE MOUNTAIN

Woody Wirt is an intrepid mountain climber. One day in southern California he went to a ski resort, told the guard he was going climbing and if he wasn't back when the ski lift stopped at five-thirty, to send someone after him.

He then rode to the top. He eventually found a chalet on the mountain and, feeling drowsy from his exertion, went inside, built a fire, and lay down for a nap.

Five-thirty came. The guard shut off the lift and routinely phoned the San Bernardino County sheriff to report that a man named Sherwood Wirt from Minneapolis, Minnesota, had not yet returned. The sheriff released the news to the press, and search parties were dispatched to find Woody.

Meanwhile, he had awakened and begun his descent. Without the aid of the ski lift, it took him about two hours to reach the bottom. Little did he know that at that moment Grady and Billy were driving toward Los Angeles, frightened out of their minds to hear a newscaster say, "A bulletin just in: Sherwood Wirt, editor of *Decision* magazine, is lost somewhere in the San Bernardino Mountains . . . ."

TIME OUT

When Lane Adams was conducting a crusade in Jefferson, Indiana, the meetings were held in Clay Park Square. The park was bounded upon one side by a superhighway and on the other by a railroad trestle. Right in the middle of Lane's sermon each evening, a switch engine would push cars across the trestle. The deafening noise ended all possibility of Lane being heard by the audience. So each evening he would stop and say,

"Wave at the engineer," which they would do, and the engineer would wave back. Then Lane would have their attention for the remainder of the evening.

RIGHT CHURCH, WRONG PEW

Mrs. Steve Robinson of Campbells Bay, Ontario, heard of a film on drugs featuring Art Linkletter and Billy Graham. She hurried to the Anglican church hall to see it and was one of the first to arrive. She noticed that the chairs were being filled mostly by men, and she wondered why these oldsters were so interested in drugs.

The group offered her coffee. Eventually it turned out that the drug film was to be shown at another Anglican church in nearby Shawville. Meanwhile, Mrs. Robinson was attending her first meeting of Alcoholics Anonymous.

THE PERSONAL TOUCH

A man asked Dr. Charles Allen, a friend of the team and a regular speaker at Billy Graham Schools of Evangelism, about his family.

"What is the number of your children?"

Dr. Allen said, "My children don't have numbers, they have names."

HEAVENLY DICTATION

At a ministers' meeting in England, John Dillon, an assistant to George Wilson in the Minneapolis office, was asked to lead in prayer.

John, unaccustomed to praying before such a prestigious group, prayed with considerable fervor. Instead of concluding his prayer in the customary manner, he was so carried away he said, "Sincerely yours, John Dillon."

A SMALL MATTER

One night during the Atlanta crusade in June, 1973, Billy confided to the audience: "I have a new suit on, and the waist is two inches too large—I want you to pray for me, because I don't have a belt on tonight."

WAKE UP!

When John Wesley White was preaching in a high school in Taegu, Korea, some of the schoolchildren fell asleep. The principal spent his time walking the aisle shaking heads "like he was twirling bowling balls," John says, and admonishing, "This man is telling us the greatest thing we have ever heard, and you have to go to sleep!"

A CHARMING MOTHER

When Billy Graham's mother was specially honored by President Nixon at a White House service, one team member said to her, "Mother Graham, now I know where Billy and the other children get all their graciousness and charm."

Mrs. Graham, who had just recently celebrated her eightieth birthday, answered with a wry smile, "Did you ever have any doubt about it?"

WHERE'S THE QUEEN?

Russell Busby, official photographer for the team, was attending a VIP dinner in Britain. He was tired and hungry, so he decided to have a good meal and not worry about taking pictures. Totally engrossed in eating, he was astounded when the master of ceremonies arose and said, "Ladies and gentlemen, I propose a toast to her majesty, the queen." Russell ran madly to get his camera, wondering why he hadn't been informed that the queen was expected—only to find, to his chagrin, that it was the usual honorary "absentee toast."

THE RUFFIANS

In the early days when Billy, Cliff, and T. W. Wilson were barnstorming for Youth for Christ under the direction of Torrey Johnson, they always had to share a room. One time, Billy returned in the wee hours of the morning from a long trip. It had been a difficult assignment. All the way back to Chicago, he had looked forward to a soft bed and some sleep as a partial reward for what he considered a wasted night.

When he arrived in his room, which was already occupied by Cliff, he saw that Cliff had all the blankets, including the bedspread, wrapped around him and was sleeping soundly in his third of the bed...the middle. Cliff's body angled back with his stomach protruding. Billy surveyed the "full" bed for a moment. Then, doubling his fist, he took a big swing and clouted Cliff in his abdomen.

It was too much for the old bed. It fell down with a bang.

Cliff awakened wide-eyed and a little vexed. He picked up one of his shoes (which was within reach now that he was on the floor), took dead aim at Billy's exuberant physiogomy, and hit the bull's-eye. With that, they both doubled over laughing.

It wasn't until later, when Billy climbed into his bed on the floor, that he learned why Cliff was under the blankets and not between the sheets. Earlier in the day, T. W. and Cliff had short-sheeted their bed for Billy's benefit.

HER OWN CONGREGATION

When Ruth Graham gave one of her talks to a Christian women's club, a lady said to her afterward, "Mrs. Graham, you're a good speaker. You should have a congregation of your own."

"I do," Ruth answered with a smile, "—my five children!"

DON'T GO NEAR THE WATER

In the spring of 1971, Leighton Ford was conducting a crusade in Philadelphia. In one of his sermons he attempted to illustrate faith. "Take a man who is thirsty," he said. "Someone may hand him a glass of water, analyze what is in it, and describe its chemical make-up; but unless he takes the glass and drinks it he will remain thirsty. It is possible to study the life of Christ and theologize about Him; but unless we receive Him into our lives we will remain empty."

Later that evening, as the crowds were dispersing, Larry Selig, director for the crusade, overheard two Philadelphians talking. "Remember that story he told about analyzing what's in a glass of water?"

"Yea," replied the second. "He doesn't know much about Philadelphia water, does he? Nobody can analyze the stuff in our water."

"That's right," said the first man, "and no Philadelphian would ever drink it if he had anything else to drink, either."

GOVERNOR, I'M TOO BUSY

In 1948 the long-time pastor of First Baptist Church of Minneapolis, Dr. W.B. Riley, who was on his deathbed, bequeathed the presidency of Northwestern Schools to Billy.

Billy soon applied to the Federal Communications Commission for an AM-FM radio station in connection with the college. The governor of Minnesota, Luther Youngdahl, graciously consented to drop by Billy's office and deliver a five-minute tape recording for the new voice of Northwestern Schools. Billy knew he was coming, but forgot it. When the governor finally arrived, George Wilson rapped on the door and said, "Governor Youngdahl is here."

Billy thought it was another joke and facetiously said, "Tell the governor I'm too busy to see him." But George insisted that the governor was actually in the office, and to prove it he opened the door. There stood the state's first citizen in the flesh. A red-faced Billy Graham stammered his apologies.

ONE IS ENOUGH

When Howard Jones was preaching in Nigeria, a Muslim leader came to him and asked, "How many wives do you have?"

Howard informed him that he had only one, and he considered one sufficient.

The Muslim then said, "That's the trouble with you Christians. You're too cheap. A man needs several wives to take care of his needs."

Then Howard asked, "Sir, do you have more than one wife?"

The Muslim answered that he had four.

"I'll bet you have a lot of wife-palaver," Howard countered.

The Muslim reflected a moment and said, "That's right, Pastor Jones, with four wives it's palaver, palaver, palaver! I guess you're right. . .a man is probably better off with one wife!"

ON PURPOSE?

During the All-Scotland Crusade in 1955, an epidemic of fainting occurred nightly in the giant, 17,500-seat Kelvin Hall. It was a familiar sight to see the first-aid attendants carrying a prone, unconscious person out of the meeting. The faintings, as many as twenty in a single evening, were a regular topic of conversation among the team. Some reasoned that the Scots could not endure the warm temperature generated by the large crowd. Others thought it might be the result of some sort of emotional stress.

Years later a team member mentioned the faintings in America, and a man from Glasgow happened to be in the audience. After the service he approached the associate and said, "Laddie, I was in attendance at the Glasgow crusade, and I can tell you why so many Scots fainted in Kelvin Hall. They fainted to keep from giving in the offering. It's an old Scottish trick," he said with a wry smile.